YOUR KNOWLEDGE HAS VALUE

- We will publish your bachelor's and master's thesis, essays and papers

- Your own eBook and book - sold worldwide in all relevant shops

- Earn money with each sale

Upload your text at www.GRIN.com
and publish for free

Bibliographic information published by the German National Library:

The German National Library lists this publication in the National Bibliography; detailed bibliographic data are available on the Internet at http://dnb.dnb.de .

This book is copyright material and must not be copied, reproduced, transferred, distributed, leased, licensed or publicly performed or used in any way except as specifically permitted in writing by the publishers, as allowed under the terms and conditions under which it was purchased or as strictly permitted by applicable copyright law. Any unauthorized distribution or use of this text may be a direct infringement of the author s and publisher s rights and those responsible may be liable in law accordingly.

Imprint:

Copyright © 2016 GRIN Verlag
Print and binding: Books on Demand GmbH, Norderstedt Germany
ISBN: 9783668642492

This book at GRIN:

https://www.grin.com/document/411978

Jan-David Franke

Aus der Reihe: e-fellows.net stipendiaten-wissen

e-fellows.net (Hrsg.)

Band 2672

Has China been socialized into international society in the post-Cold War period?

GRIN Verlag

GRIN - Your knowledge has value

Since its foundation in 1998, GRIN has specialized in publishing academic texts by students, college teachers and other academics as e-book and printed book. The website www.grin.com is an ideal platform for presenting term papers, final papers, scientific essays, dissertations and specialist books.

Visit us on the internet:

http://www.grin.com/

http://www.facebook.com/grincom

http://www.twitter.com/grin_com

W6Q1. Has China been socialized into international society in the post-Cold War period?
Jan-David Franke

With the collapse of the Soviet Union the United States benefitted from an unprecedented unipolar moment in its establishment of unilateral hegemony, be that in the form of a modern empire as Johnson (2000) and Todd (2004) argue, as an empire by invitation (Lundestad, 2003), or as liberal hegemon (Ikenberry, 2011). All of these authors feature vast disagreements regarding hierarchy and coercion in American hegemony but accept the same premise: a post-Cold War unipolar American world order. Many argue that as the unipolar moment is waning, American hegemony, and the norms, practices, and institutions of international society it has so predominantly shaped, are being challenged, however, by both the rise of other actors, first and foremost China but also a re-emerging Russia, and the endogenous deconstruction of American hegemony (see Todd's (2004) argument on demographics and social norms and most recently the advent of power by a protectionist, isolationist nativism). In this paper I will add to that debate by evaluating the extent to which China has been socialized into international society since the end of the Cold War and, on that basis, examining what is to be expected for the future both in terms of China's course and the implications thereof for international society. I will do so by amalgamating many different approaches and schools of thought in an attempt to be 'paradigmatically prudent' (cp. Monteiro & Ruby, 2009). First, I will sketch the discussion in the literature on China's rise and contrast it by means of a syncretic framework of intentions and outcomes based on Schweller & Xiaoyu (2011) and Goh (2005). Within that framework, I present optimist and pessimist approaches derived from realism, liberal institutionalism, and constructivism and the various analytical categories they place emphasis on. I will then argue that an integration of these polarized perspectives is necessary to provide an accurate and realistic account of China's past, present, and future role in international society that places particular importance on differentiated spheres of geopolitical influence.

In his work that laid the foundation for the English School of IR, Bull (1977) defined three spheres, layers of normative and institutional communitization as it were, within the anarchical system. The first, the international system, is constituted by the interaction of two or more states so that the behavior of each is a necessary element in the calculations of the others (pp. 9-10). In a Realist vein, the international system is dominated by international anarchy and power politics. It is ontologically prior to international society, in which the system is augmented by shared rules and institutions which have been established by dialogue and consent and which are stabilized by a recognition that there is common interest in maintaining the arrangements they engender. In order to 'move' from the system to society level, parties must grant mutual respect and inclusion into the international society whilst honoring, above all, each other's sovereignty. In the third and last sphere, world society, a sort of Kantian liberal universalism is invoked by which an international community fulfils a common moral and political purpose and sovereignty is ceded to global governance. This differentiation is important to keep in mind throughout this paper. If I were to discuss the role of an emerging China in the international system based on the Realist-leaning English School definition of the term, then particular emphasis should be placed on the changing structures of power within it, which means exclusively scrutinizing the Chinese challenge to US unipolarity. Talking about international society, however, means we also need to look at the extent to which China has acted as a revisionist or status quo power respectively with regard to the shared rules and institutions that qualify international society, many of which have been shaped by US hegemony, and which inferences that induces vis-à-vis the future of China's role in international society. The assumption of a singular (world) international society inherent in the prompt and in the English School in general is rooted in the conventional narrative of European expansion (cp. Watson, 1985) and can therefore be rightfully criticized for excluding alternative and subaltern narratives, realities, and discourses. While a further critical examination of that bias is highly recommended but not attempted within the confines of this essay, it does inform later remarks on what the partially reciprocative nature of the examined socialization process means for the legitimacy of international order.

According to Schweller and Xiaoyu (2011) there are roughly three different paths for China's engagement with international society varying by the degree of China's socialization. Either, they argue, we have been seeing and will continue to see the conception of a new international order (perhaps in the fashion of a tributary system, cp. Khong, 2013); or China contests some rules, principles, and norms that it disagrees with while accepting, if not internalizing, others; or China is unilaterally socialized into international society and lends its support to its present structure. Goh (2005) offers a similar categorization, albeit with the emphasis not on Chinese intentions as is the case with Schweller and Xiaoyu but on strategic outcomes, which highlights the agency of the established powers in international society, most notably of course the US, in responding to China's course of action and shaping the future of international society. A combination of these two frameworks allows me to not only discuss to which extent China has been socialized into international society but also deliberate how the international society responds to Chinese emergence and how it is going to be affected by it (see Figure 1, appendix)). As Xuetong (2006, p. 5) writes "the assessment of China's present power status in the world, to a certain extent, reflects people's concern about the rise of China in the future."

Realists, in this case defensive and offensive realists as well as power transition theorists, occupy the right part of the 'intentions' spectrum (see Figure 1, appendix), assuming that China has and will continue to pursue revisionist policies that challenge American hegemony and the fabric of international society. Offensive realists like Mearsheimer (2010) posit that China will, as its power increases, act increasingly assertive and aggressive which will inevitably evoke a firm American response an thereby increase the likelihood of a Cold War standoff of hegemonic war. They point to the decisiveness of China's claims in the South China Sea and the rigor with which they have been articulated thus far. Goh (2005) categorizes this perspective as 'Scenario D', in which no power sharing occurs as Chinese power accumulation proceeds. Power Transition Theory initially formulated by Organski (1958) goes even one step further, positing that as the great power China challenges the (retrenching) hegemonic US, a major war is more or less inevitable that will eventually effect a transition of hegemonic power to China (see Goh, 2005; Tammen & Kugler, 2006). In consequence, that means that China reshapes international society to its own liking rather than be socialized into it. Defensive realists like Glaser (2011) agree that China's growing military capabilities are going hand in hand with a challenge to US hegemony and international order, however, they take a less pessimistic stance on the implications of that with regards to both the aggressiveness with which China will attempt to revise principles of international society as well as the response by the United States. Great importance is attributed to reliable signaling and greater and more transparent information about respective intentions if conflict is to be avoided. Glaser recommends for the US to make adjustments to its security policies regarding 'less-than-vital interests' in order to strike a peaceful compromise with ascending China and considers strategic variables like nuclear weapons and geographical distance to be vital security guarantors. Glaser therefore does not exclude the possibility of a 'hierarchical duet' (cp. Goh, 2005), given that the US does not retaliate all too dogmatically against China's rise.

The Realist perspective is opposed by liberal institutionalists which "argue that because the current international order is defined by economic and political openness, it can accommodate China's rise peacefully. The United States and other leading powers, this argument runs, can and will make clear that China is welcome to join the existing order and prosper within it, and China is likely to do so rather than launch a costly and dangerous struggle to overturn the system and establish an order more to its own liking." (Glaser, 2011, para. 3). According to Economy and Oksenberg (1999), China has become a more responsible stakeholder in international society, having joined almost all international regimes and institutions, even those that it previously considered tools of US hegemony, including the Bretton Woods institutions and the WTO. While its participation in these regimes is often reluctant, especially in contexts that it considers a solidarist intrusion into its pluralist principles (above all national sovereignty), there is reason to believe that the Chinese government is increasingly accepting elements of solidarism as it recognizes the economic, political, and reputational gains from doing so. Liberal institutionalists might have a hard time explaining, however, why in 2015 China established the Asian Infrastructure Investment Bank as a purposeful alternative to the

Bretton Woods institutions which it claims to be dominated by Western interests. After all, this raises doubt on Economy and Oksenberg's prediction that China will become an increasingly active and positive part of traditional international regimes, especially in a regional context.

One might be inclined to believe that the apparent divide between conflict and status quo, socialization and polarization, pessimism and optimism, liberalism and realism is best bridged by resorting to constructivist perspectives. After all, constructivists cover the whole spectrum from revisionist/conflictual to status quo, as their emphasis is on interaction and consequent identity and norm negotiation as the organizing principle when analyzing the rise of China in international society. Depending on the conclusions drawn from the perceptual and ideational factors constructivist scholars emphasize, they can be arranged from optimist to pessimist constructivists along both the intensions and outcome axes (Friedberg, 2005). Optimistic constructivists like Johnston (2008) believe that as China interacts with liberal institutions in international society it is socialized into their liberal norms, identities, and strategic cultures. Friedberg (2005) points out that while liberal institutionalists pay particular attention to "the role of institutions in altering the narrow cost-benefit calculations of rational decisionmakers, constructivists believe that repeated interactions can actually change the underlying beliefs, interests, and mental categories of those who participate in them" (p. 35). Pessimistic constructivists like Berger (2000) on the other side fear that repeated interaction, instead of leading to unilateral socialization, will reinforce contrary identities as well as foster mutual understanding thereof. The US will continue to regard China as dangerous and its regime as illegitimate, China on the other side will continue to consider American involvement in the region as intrusive and aggressive. Accordingly, the skepticism with which China treats US-championed human rights-related norms (let alone humanitarian intervention) and democracy (see Lynch, 2006, p. 16) is an indication of that scenario.

It becomes apparent that while pessimistic and optimistic constructivism expand the analytical scope of liberalist and realist perspectives in valuable ways by adding the negotiation of identity and norms through continuous interaction, they, too, do not capture the vast area in the middle of the intension/outcome framework (see Figure 1, appendix). As Friedberg (2005) rightly observes in the context of the debate on China, "driven by the desire to construct parsimonious theories and to establish the preponderance of one paradigm or school, scholars have often been inclined to adopt an all-or- nothing attitude, asserting the overwhelming importance of the causal mechanisms central to their preferred paradigm while downplaying or ignoring the possible significance of others" (p. 10). In order to redress that problem, I argue for a rejection, or rather an integration, of pessimistic and optimistic categories in favor of a realistic constructivism (or 'realism', not to be confused with the IR paradigm) that salvages relevant perspectives and insights from both liberal institutionalism and realism. Differentiating levels of analysis by spheres of influence, as to "maintain political plurality against universalizing tendencies" (Hast, 2014, p. 45) is particularly useful in that respect. Both optimistic and pessimistic approaches fall prey to confirmation bias when it comes to evaluating empirical instances of Chinese behavior in international society, with pessimists being aided by looking at the South China Sea and Taiwan flashpoints as well as the establishment of the Asian Infrastructure Investment Bank and optimists focusing on China's engagement in multilateral institutions like the UN, ASEAN, the WTO or the Comprehensive Test Ban Treaty (see Friedberg, 2005, p. 36). In fact, as Zhang (2016) points out, China's course since the end of the cold war is characterized by "a range of preferences for the normative change of international society on the pluralism-solidarism spectrum" (p. 816) with a deeply rooted pluralist identity on the one side which it is not willing to give up and a moderate openness to solidarist values in global governance on the other side that derive from its entanglement with liberal hierarchy in global international society. What can be drawn from Zhang's work, albeit not explicitly addressed by him, is that China's behavior is best understood when controlling for spheres of influence. On the global stage, there is indeed reason to believe that, as Zhang observes, China displays a certain degree of flexibility, both out of self-interest (as liberal institutionalists allege) and through a partial socialization into the strategic culture of international society (as optimistic constructivists claim). China's recent contributions to UN peacekeeping missions (Fung, 2016) bear testimony to that flexibility (Fung, 2016). In turn, China by virtue of its powerful position in the UN Security Council and other corridors of institutional power also exercises agency in the evolution of global order by promoting a flexible pluralist state-centric approach. That is true especially when matters of regional interest to China, or principles to which China prefers to take regional exception, become elevated into a universal or global argument, manifest, amongst other things, in China's rejection of the UNCLOS Tribunal regarding freedom of navigation in the South China Sea (see Khurana, 2016). Rather than effecting the reinforcement of contrary identities on the one side or allowing a unilateral socialization into liberal hegemony on the other side, China has been and will continue to accept and internalize parts of the principles of international society while challenging and transforming others. China socializes into international society while international society becomes more Chinese. As Kissinger of all people (1964, pp. 1-2) points out, the legitimacy of international order depends on that level of mutual convergence. In a regional context, however, China has shown a far more revisionist line of action. In fact, most empirical arguments made by pessimists in the debate, such as the aforementioned South China Sea, Taiwan, and the Asian Infrastructure Investment Bank, relate to Chinese efforts of 'East Asian regionalization' (see Xuetong, 2005, p. 33) and not primarily in global international society. It appears that while partially abiding by the rules of the game on the global level, China is keen to construct various regional regimes when it comes to security, economic development, and international law. Its previous engagement in regional institutions like ASEAN gives reason to believe that, even in the regional context, this line of action will not be as assertive or aggressive as offensive realists would expect. Nonetheless, the main *direct* conflict potential does not necessarily arise from its relationship with the Western powers, the US above all, but from regional institutional and strategic flashpoints. After all, the Asian Infrastructure Investment Bank was not only established in opposition to the Bretton Woods institutions but also the Asian Development Bank which China claims to be dominated by Japanese interests. To the extent that the institutional setup of international society and the United States will allow for it, a hierarchical duet constitutes the most realistic summation of possible intentions and outcomes, by which China is not only integrated into global international society while transforming it at the same time in a process of mutual convergence of principles and interests but also carves out a regional space in which it seeks to construct partially hegemonic regimes. In fact, much will depend on how China's regional competitors, most importantly South Korea, Japan, and the Philippines, react to that and – and this is where the key role of the US lies – in how far they can rely on their strategic alliance with the United States.

Conclusion

As Xuetong (2006) observes, "scholars still have not reached any agreement on China's power status today" (p. 5), let alone on what is to be expected for its course in international society and the implications thereof for international order. In this paper, I have presented the prevalent debate on whether China has been, or is, socialized into international society and which expectations that allows for the future. To that end, I have employed a syncretic framework of intentions and outcomes based on Schweller and Xiaoyu (2011) and Goh (2005), depicted in Figure 1 (appendix). Realists, especially offensive realists and power transition theorists, are quite pessimistic about the integration of China into a US-dominated international society, holding war to be likely if not evitable. Defensive realists place more emphasis on the reaction of the US to the Chinese challenge and the role of signaling, thereby offering the possibility of a non-conflictual hierarchical duet. Pessimistic constructivists believe that as China continues to interact with a liberal institutions, contrary identities on both sides will be reinforced and normative and political fronts will be hardened. Liberal institutionalists, on the other side, make the case for the rational power of institutions in which China can prosper and through which China, despite its pluralist reservations, has become a responsible stakeholder with a direct interest in the maintenance of stability. Optimistic constructivists go even step further by alleging that China, its identity, norms, and strategic culture, have been gradually socialized into international society by virtue of repeated intra- and extra-institutional interaction with the liberal order. In order to bridge the argumentative gap that is left open by both pessimists and optimists, I have argued for a realistic account of China's rise that integrates the various approaches and emphasizes mutual convergence in international society on the global scale and partial revisionism in China's regional sphere of influence (see Figure 1, appendix). In light of policy implications that are derived from an academic analysis on China's relationship with international society, it appears imperative not to under- or overstate the dangers of China's rise and not to ignore various geopolitical spheres of influence. That is especially relevant given that just over two months from now an administration is going to take office in the United States that is ignorant at best and jingoist at worst when China's role in international society is concerned.

Bibliography

Berger, T. (2000) Set for stability? Prospects for conflict and cooperation in East Asia. *Review of International Studies, 26*(3), 405-428.

Bull, H. (1977). *The anarchical society*. New York City, NY: Columbia University Press.

Clark, I. (2011). China and the United States: a succession of hegemonies? *International Affairs, 87*(1), 13-28.

Economy, E., & Oksenberg, M. (1999). *China joins the world: progress and prospects*. New York: Council on Foreign Relations Press.

Foot, R. (2002). Introduction. In R. Foot, J. Gaddis & A. Hurrell (Eds.), *Order and Justice in International Relations* (pp. 1-32). Oxford: Oxford University Press.

Friedberg, A. (2005). The future of U.S.-China relations: is conflict inevitable? *International Security, 30*(2), 7-45.

Fung, C. (2016, July 26). China's troop contributions to U.N. peacekeeping. *United States Institute of Peace*. Retrieved from http://www.usip.org/publications/2016/07/26/china-s-troop-contributions-un-peacekeeping

Glaser, C. (2011). Will China's rise lead to war? Why realism does not mean pessimism. *Foreign Affairs, 90*(2), 80-91.

Goh, E. (2005). The U.S.-China relationship and Asia-Pacific security: negotiating change. *Asian Security, 1*(3), 216-244.

Hast, S. (2014). *Spheres of influence in international relations: history, theory and politics*. London: Routledge.

Ikenberry, J. (2011). *Liberal leviathan: the origins, crisis, and transformation of the American world order*. Princeton, NJ: Princeton University Press.

Johnson, C. (2000). *Blowback: the costs and consequences of American empire*. NY: Owl Books.

Johnston, A. (2008). *Social states: China in international institutions, 1980-2000*. Princeton, NJ: Princeton University Press.

Khurana, G. (2016, August 19). China and freedom of navigation: the context of the international tribunal's verdict. *Center for International Maritime Security*. Retrieved from http://cimsec.org/china-freedom-navigation-south-china-sea-context-international-tribunals-verdict/27336

Kissinger, H. (1964). *A world restored*. New York: Grossett & Dunlap.

Khong, Y. (2013). The American tributary system. *The Chinese Journal of International Politics, 6*(1), 1-48.

Lundestad, G. (2003). *The United States and Western Europe since 1945*. Oxford: Oxford University Press.

Lynch, D. (2006). *Rising China and Asian democratization: socialization to "global culture" in in the political transformations of Thailand, China, and Taiwan*. Stanford, CA: Stanford University Press.

Mearsheimer, J. (2010). The gathering storm: China's challenge to US power in Asia," *The Chinese Journal of International Politics, (3)*4, 381-96.

Monteiro, N., & Ruby, K. (2009). IR and the false promise of philosophical foundations. *International Theory, 1*(1), 15-48.

Organski, A. (1958). *World Politics*. New York: Knopf.

Schweller, R., & Xiaoyu, P. (2011). After unipolarity: China's visions of international order in an era of U.S. decline. *International Security, 36*(1), 41-72.

Tammen, R., & Kugler, J. (2006). Power transition and China-US conflicts. *Chinese Journal of International Politics, 1*, 35-55.

Todd, E. (2004). *After the empire: the breakdown of American order*. NY: Columbia University Press.

Watson, A. (1985). European international society and its expansion. In H. Bull & A. Watson (Eds.), *The expansion of international society* (pp. 13-32) . Oxford: Oxford University Press.

Xuetong, Y. (2005). The rise of China and its power status. *Chinese Journal of International Politics, 1*, 5-33.

Appendix

Figure 1: **A Framework for China & International Society**

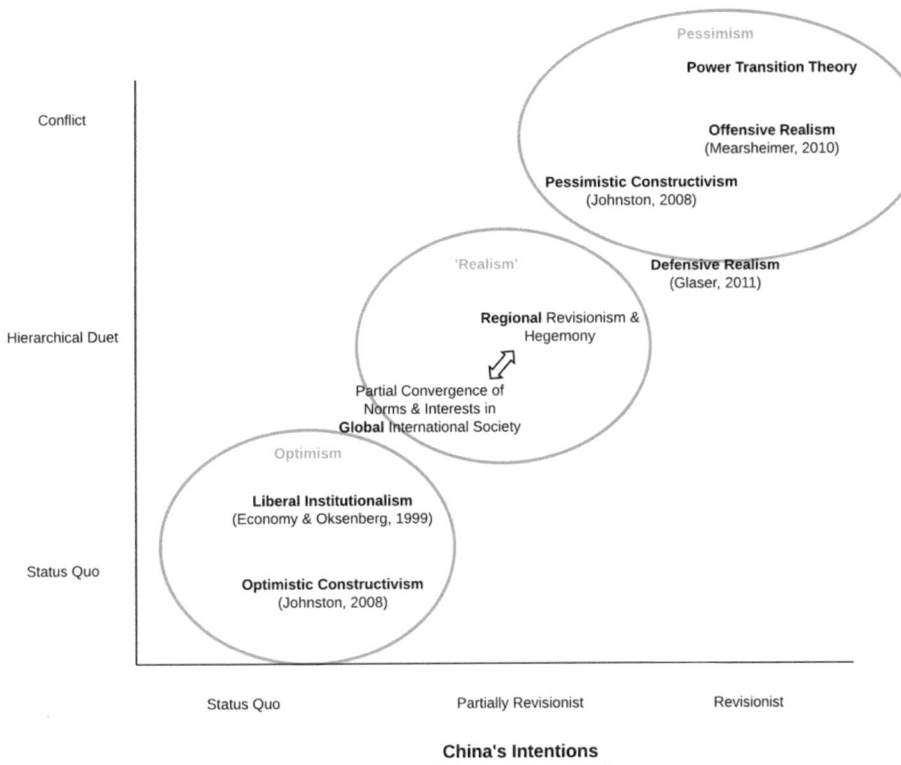

YOUR KNOWLEDGE HAS VALUE

- We will publish your bachelor's and master's thesis, essays and papers

- Your own eBook and book - sold worldwide in all relevant shops

- Earn money with each sale

Upload your text at www.GRIN.com
and publish for free